SUSAN E. GOODMAN
ILLUSTRATED BY E. B. LEWIS

The First Step

How One Girl Put Segregation on Trial

BLOOMSBURY

NEW YORK LONDON OXFORD NEW DELHI SYDNEY

Acknowledgments

Thanks to all who lent information and perspective: David Elliott; Deborah Hirschland; Paul Kendrick; Cheryl Brown Henderson; Lena Reddick; Franklin A. Dorman; Emily Novak Gustainis at Historic New England; Carole Doody at the Social Law Library; Anna J. Clutterbuck-Cook at the Massachusetts Historical Society; Laura E. Wasowicz at the American Antiquarian Society; Lonnie G. Bunch, director of the Smithsonian National Museum of African American History and Culture; as well as the staffs of the Boston City, Massachusetts State, and Massachusetts Supreme Judicial Court Archives; Boston's Museum of African American History; Leventhal Map Center; and the National Park Service. Special thanks to all the amazing people at Bloomsbury. And then there's E. B. Lewis.

First published in the United States of America in January 2016 by Bloomsbury Children's Books
www.bloomsbury.com

Bloomsbury is a registered trademark of Bloomsbury Publishing Plc

For information about permission to reproduce selections from this book, write to
Permissions, Bloomsbury Children's Books, 1385 Broadway, New York, New York 10018
Bloomsbury books may be purchased for business or promotional use. For information on bulk purchases
please contact Macmillan Corporate and Premium Sales Department at specialmarkets@macmillan.com

Library of Congress Cataloging-in-Publication Data
Goodman, Susan E.
The first step : how one girl put segregation on trial / by Susan E. Goodman ; illustrated by E.B. Lewis.
pages   cm
ISBN 978-0-8027-3739-7 (hardcover) • ISBN 978-0-8027-3741-0 (e-book) • ISBN 978-0-8027-3742-7 (e-PDF)
1. Roberts, Sarah C., 1844—Trials, litigation, etc.—Juvenile literature. 2. Segregation in education—Law and legislation—Massachusetts—Boston—Juvenile literature. 3. Discrimination in education—Law and legislation—Massachusetts—Boston—Juvenile literature. 4. African Americans—Education—Massachusetts—Juvenile literature. 5. African Americans—Legal status, laws, etc.—United States—Juvenile literature. 6. Segregation in education—Law and legislation—United States—Juvenile literature. I. Lewis, Earl B., illustrator. II. Title.
KF228.R56G66 2016   344.744'0798—dc23   2015008527

Art created with watercolors and gouache on 300-pound Arches hot press paper
Typeset in Goudy Old Style • Book design by Ellice M. Lee

Printed in China by Leo Paper Products, Heshan, Guangdong
1 3 5 7 9 10 8 6 4 2

To Mari and Vivian:
We're all part of the walk.
March on.
—S. E. G.

To Bernadette Santiago, whom I adore
—E. B. L.

Sarah Roberts was four years old when she started school in April 1847. Even though it was spring, icy winds still wailed off Boston Harbor near Sarah's home. She was lucky her school was so close by.

Sarah dashed past the hay sellers and carpenters, the organ makers and oystermen. After crossing Causeway Street, she was just steps from the Otis School.

The Otis was one of Boston's best, with more books than most kids had ever seen.

Sarah practiced her sums and letters. She memorized poems. She spent recess in the play yard with her classmates.

Then one day, a policeman walked into Sarah's classroom. He took her out of her school and said she could never come back. Ever.

The Otis School was only for white children.

Sarah must have been surprised and frightened when she was forced out onto the sidewalk. But Boston had a rule that said African American children must go to a separate school just for them.

Sarah's parents hated this unfair decree and had enrolled her in the
Otis anyway. Once the people in charge of city schools realized what
had happened, they threw Sarah out.

Her parents weren't surprised or frightened. They were angry.

Adeline and Benjamin Roberts tried to imagine Sarah's walk to the Smith School, which was for African American children. She would have to zigzag through many streets, crossing one neighborhood after another.

Sarah would have to go all that way for a school that never taught subjects like history or drawing. All that way for Boston's only school without a play yard. A school that owned only one book.

Every day Sarah would pass one . . . two . . . three . . . four . . . five schools she could not enter.

Sarah's father had taken this trip when he was a boy. He knew exactly how it felt to look up at all those windows filled with white children. And how it felt when the children looked down on him.

No child should ever feel that way again, certainly not his Sarah.

Her parents stepped up to fight for change.

Sarah's great-grandfather was a soldier in the Revolutionary War, fighting to free Americans from unfair laws. Sarah needed a different kind of warrior this time—one whose battlefield was a courtroom, a lawyer fighting to convince judges that this rule must be changed.

Sarah's parents picked Robert Morris to be her champion. Morris was the second African American lawyer in the entire United States. He was new at his job; in fact, he had taken only one case to court before. But he had won.

It took Morris more than two years to get Sarah's case to the most powerful court in Massachusetts. He knew it was her only chance of winning.

As Sarah's trial grew near, Robert Morris asked another lawyer to join him. Charles Sumner despised the way his country treated African Americans. What's more, he had a special gift. He was a great speaker. When Sumner talked about justice, he could touch people's hearts.

On December 4, 1849, a heavy snow blanketed the city. Even a ferocious blizzard wouldn't have stopped people from flooding into the courthouse. So many of them were African American—dockworkers and washerwomen, barbers and blacksmiths—giving up a day's pay to be there. Some were lucky enough to get a seat. Others were willing to stand, for hours if need be.

Sarah's story was their story too.

Her case seemed to be changing things already. It was the first case asking our legal system to outlaw separate schools. It was the first time an African American lawyer argued before a supreme court. It was also the first time an African American lawyer and a white lawyer teamed up to fight for justice.

Three important steps forward.

Sarah and her family sat in front, dressed in their finest. Spectators buzzed all around them until the judges filed in and were seated.

Robert Morris had been Sarah's voice from the beginning. He spoke first here too. He presented the facts of her case, including the two most important: Boston's rule said students should go to schools nearest their homes. Yet Sarah's skin color meant she must cross the city to reach hers.

Anyone looking at Sarah could imagine how long that journey would feel. In a grown-up's chair, her legs were too short to reach the floor.

Charles Sumner's long speech lay on the table, but he barely looked at it as he spoke.

"'All men are created equal,' says the Declaration of Independence," Sumner stated. "'All men are born free and equal,' says the Massachusetts Bill of Rights. Education in Boston is brought to every white man's door. But it is not brought to every black man's door. He is obliged to go for it—to travel for it—to walk for it—often a great distance."

Even worse, Sumner said, African American children are forced into a school for themselves alone. Any school that sets a race apart cannot be as good as one where all children come together as equals. Equals, as promised by Massachusetts law.

Sumner's clear voice rang through the courtroom. "This little child asks at your hands her personal rights."

Everyone knew that if Sarah got her rights, so would every other African American child in Boston.

After four long months, the judges announced their decision.

All that work, all that hope, and Sarah had lost. It was a giant step backward.

So many people felt angry and helpless, because the judgment was final . . .

. . . for the time being.

Every big change has to start somewhere.

Sarah's father crossed the state asking people to sign petitions that said all children—no matter the color of their skin—should be able to attend their neighborhood schools. Sarah's story inspired other African Americans to push for their rights. People passed around copies of Charles Sumner's speech. They started using an important new phrase: "equality before the law."

More petitions went out; more names flooded in. When all these demands were delivered to the State House, politicians began talking too.

Sarah's case had lost in court, but her cause was won when people—black *and* white—stood together and said . . .

No more. Now, right now, it is time for change!

In 1855, Boston stepped into the history books as the first major American city to officially integrate its schools. Over time, other cities followed Boston's example.

Not all of them, though. They didn't have to. Back then, every state could make its own laws about this issue.

The march toward justice is a long, twisting journey.
Three steps forward, one step back.
One step forward, three back.

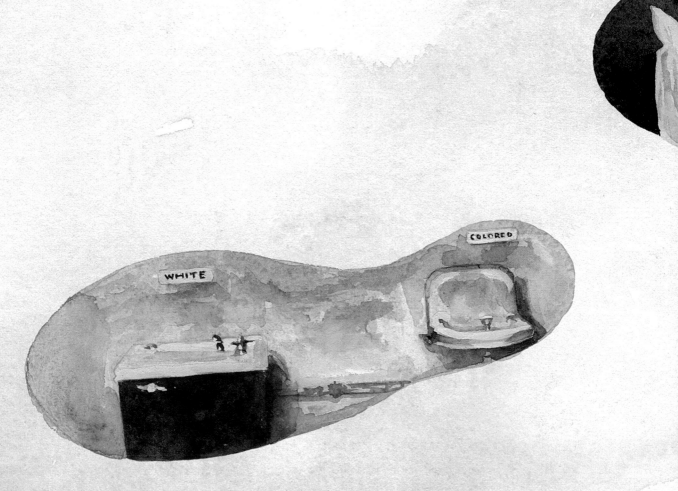

Laws change, and the march moves forward.

People resist change, and the march slows to a standstill, waiting for a better time.

Then, at last, ideas have changed enough and people have changed enough. Finally the march cannot be stopped.

In 1950, about one hundred years after Sarah's legal defeat, another girl and her family said, *No more!*

Eight-year-old Linda Brown had to cross a dangerous train yard in Topeka, Kansas, walk six blocks to a bus stop, then ride all the way to her elementary school.

A better school—named, oddly enough, after Charles Sumner—was a mere seven blocks from her home. It was for white children only.

This time, however, the Brown family was one of two hundred families from several states who joined together to stop segregation in schools for the whole country. They were organized by a group called the NAACP (National Association for the Advancement of Colored People). All these people worked together for years, joining the spirit of everyone who had fought for this cause in the past century.

This time the case was heard by the country's most powerful court, the Supreme Court of the United States.

On May 17, 1954, the US Supreme Court announced its decision. All nine judges agreed with Charles Sumner. Separating children "because of their race generates a feeling of inferiority . . . that may affect their hearts and minds in a way unlikely to ever be undone."

Separate schools can never be equal, declared the judges. They must be outlawed in every state of the land.

"*It is so ordered.*"

When the gavel slammed down to end court that day, it announced change all over the country. And in its echo, you could hear the sound of Sarah's first steps to school and her long road to justice.

Marching toward Equality

In 1954, *Brown v. Board of Education* declared that segregation was against the law. More than sixty years later, we've seen progress in so many areas of American society—including the election of our first African American president. Yet public schools are more segregated than they were in 1970. The road to justice is a long, twisting journey.

This timeline lists many of the ideas and events that have brought us to where we are today. Some people will see a specific incident as progress. Others will not. *Read them and decide for yourself: Is this a step forward? Or a step back?*

1848 • Benjamin Roberts files *Roberts v. City of Boston*, the first step toward turning the idea of desegregating schools into law.

1850 • The Massachusetts Supreme Court says segregated schools are legal.

1855 • Boston is the first major city to officially integrate its schools.

1863 • President Lincoln's Emancipation Proclamation frees all Southern slaves.

1865 • Abraham Lincoln is assassinated.
• The Ku Klux Klan (KKK), a group using violence to fight civil rights, is founded.

1865–1870 • The Thirteenth Amendment ends slavery; the Fourteenth Amendment makes African Americans born in the United States citizens with equal rights under the law; the Fifteenth Amendment guarantees US male citizens the right to vote, regardless of race.

1875 • A year after Charles Sumner's death, his bill, the Civil Rights Act of 1875, becomes law.

1877 • Southern states begin passing Jim Crow laws that continued to oppress African American rights and enforce segregation until the mid-twentieth century.

1883 • The US Supreme Court declares the Civil Rights Act of 1875 unconstitutional.

1896 • In its *Plessy v. Ferguson* decision, the US Supreme Court says "separate but equal" is constitutional.

1909 • The NAACP is founded to work for civil rights.

1920 • The Nineteenth Amendment gives US female citizens the right to vote, regardless of race.

1941 • President Franklin D. Roosevelt issues an executive order against "discrimination in the employment of workers in defense industries or Government."
• The US Army Air Forces creates Tuskegee Army Air Field, the first facility to train African American fighter pilots; it is a segregated base.

An Integration Timeline

1943 • African American and white college students stage the first lunch-counter sit-in at a Chicago coffee shop, which becomes an integrated restaurant.

1947 • A federal court bans segregated schools for Mexican American and white students in California.

• Jackie Robinson integrates Major League Baseball.

1948 • President Truman orders the desegregation of the United States military.

1949 • The Air Force leads the US Armed Forces by integrating its units.

1954 • In its *Brown v. Board of Education* decision, the US Supreme Court makes school segregation unconstitutional, saying separate is never equal.

1957 • President Eisenhower sends federal troops to protect nine African American teens, who integrate Central High School in Little Rock, Arkansas.

1959 • 26,000 young people march in Washington, DC, to support school integration.

• Prince Edward County, Virginia, closes its public schools to avoid integrating them.

1960 • Ruby Bridges, Tessie Prevost, Gail Etienne, and Leona Tate become the first African American children to integrate an elementary school.

1964 • The US Supreme Court orders Prince Edward County to open integrated schools.

• The Civil Rights Act is passed. Echoing many of Sumner's ideas, it bans segregation in public places, discrimination by employers, and federal support of biased programs.

1967 • General counsel of the NAACP Thurgood Marshall becomes the US Supreme Court's first African American justice.

1971 • The US Supreme Court approves busing to keep segregated communities from having segregated schools.

1973 • Thousands of white Bostonians demonstrate to protest "forced busing."

1995 • The US Supreme Court sets a goal to return control of schools to local governments so they can create their own desegregation plans.

2003 • Harvard University's Civil Rights Project finds that US schools are more segregated in 2000 than they were in 1970 when busing for desegregation began.

2007 • In its *Parents Involved* decision, the US Supreme Court says that using race as the only reason for school assignments is unconstitutional.

2008 • Barack Obama is the first African American to be elected president of the United States.

2014 • The United States marks the sixtieth anniversary of *Brown v. Board of Education*.

What Happened to Our Heroes?

ROBERT MORRIS After Sarah's case, Robert Morris kept fighting for civil rights in court, and even in the streets. When a new US law said escaped slaves could be seized and returned, no matter how long they'd lived up North, Morris did more than give legal advice. Once, he led a mob that rescued a recaptured slave, then smuggled him to freedom on the Underground Railroad. President Millard Fillmore insisted Morris and others be tried for treason—a crime that could be punished by death. Morris was freed, in part because an unexpected witness stood up for him at his trial. It was Chief Justice Lemuel Shaw, the judge who ruled against him in the *Roberts* case. Years later, Morris occasionally served as a judge himself in Boston area courts. He was the first African American lawyer to file a lawsuit, work on an integrated legal team, and become a judge.

CHARLES SUMNER Sumner was elected a Massachusetts senator and brought the ideas and arguments he formed for Sarah's case to Washington, DC. In 1856 he insulted two Southern senators in a fiery speech against slavery. Soon after, a Southern congressman took revenge by bashing Sumner on the head with his gold-topped cane. Trapped at his desk, Sumner could not defend himself and was beaten until the cane splintered into pieces. He was so physically and emotionally wounded, he could not return to work for three years. Massachusetts voters reelected him anyway. Even his empty seat was a powerful symbol of his fight against slavery. Sumner was a senator for twenty-three years, until he died in 1874.

BENJAMIN ROBERTS After Sarah's case was lost, her father traveled around Massachusetts with a runaway slave named Henry Brown. Brown told his story about escaping slavery by being sealed in a box and mailed to freedom. (A book about Brown, *Henry's Freedom Box*, is listed in the bibliography.) Roberts talked about race relations and Sarah's case. He also collected some of the petition signatures that helped integrate Boston's schools. After that victory, Roberts went back to being a printer and writing newspaper articles.

SARAH ROBERTS History is usually written about people who have power. In the mid-1800s that group rarely included African American women and children. So it isn't surprising that we don't know much about Sarah's mother, Adeline. Even though Sarah's name appears in legal history books, we know so little about her too. We do know Sarah was going to school in the nearby town of Cambridge by the time Boston schools were finally integrated. And as a teenager, she lived with her grandfather for a while. But what did Sarah think about being part of her father's dream for change? How did she feel about being the center of all that attention? How did it affect her life as she grew older? We can only imagine.

Sources and Resources

Just a few sources I used to research *The First Step*

Books

Jacobs, Donald M., ed. *Courage and Conscience: Black and White Abolitionists in Boston.* Indianapolis: Indiana University Press, 1993.

Kendrick, Stephen, and Paul Kendrick. *Sarah's Long Walk: The Free Blacks of Boston and How Their Struggle for Equality Changed America.* Boston: Beacon Press, 2004.

Stewart, James Brewer. *Abolitionist Politics and the Coming of the Civil War.* Amherst: University of Massachusetts Press, 2008.

Primary sources

The Boston Directory, Boston, George Adams, Publisher and Proprietor, 1849.

Roberts v. City of Boston court records: www.blackpast.org

Charles Sumner's speech: www.blackpast.org

Websites

Brown Foundation for Educational Equity, Excellence, and Research: www.brownvboard.org

Massachusetts Historical Society—Long Road to Justice: www.masshist.org/longroad/02education/education.htm

Teaching Tolerance: www.tolerance.org

Kids.gov: www.kids.usa.gov/history

History for Kids: www.ducksters.com/history

Documentary videos

The Road to Brown. Produced, directed, and written by William Elwood. San Francisco: California Newsreel, 1989.

Beyond Brown: Pursuing the Promise. Executive producers: Stanley Nelson and Marcia A. Smith. New York City: Firelight Media, 2004.

Professional authors aren't the only ones who do research—you kids can too; start with the websites and videos listed above and read these nonfiction books for kids

Coles, Robert. *The Story of Ruby Bridges.* New York: Scholastic, 1995.

Lester, Julius. *Let's Talk About Race.* New York: HarperCollins, 2005.

Levine, Ellen. *Henry's Freedom Box: A True Story from the Underground Railroad.* New York: Scholastic, 2007.

Tonatiuh, Duncan. *Separate Is Never Equal: Sylvia Mendez and Her Family's Fight for Desegregation.* New York: Harry N. Abrams, 2014.

Fiction can help teach history too; here are some books to get you started

Conkling, Winifred. *Sylvia and Aki.* New York: Random House Children's Books, 2013.

Levine, Kristin. *The Lions of Little Rock.* New York: G. P. Putnam's Sons, 2012.

Littlesugar, Amy. *Freedom School, Yes!* New York: Philomel, 2001.

Woodson, Jacqueline. *The Other Side.* New York: G. P. Putnam's Sons, 2001.

Author's Note

Writing Nonfiction; Writing about Sarah

Nonfiction authors feel a special responsibility when writing about other people. We're telling *their* story, after all. And if they lived long ago, they aren't around to clear up mistakes. Nevertheless, telling the truth means finding the facts *and* the emotional truths. Sarah's story was hard because we know a lot about her trial but very little about her as a person.

Gathering Facts from Places We Trust

Boston is my home, so I walked many streets in this story, especially the cobblestoned ones that feel as if they could lead back to 1847. But time has changed other parts of Sarah's Boston. Her street has been swallowed up by a huge office building, and part of the nearby harbor has been filled in to become Boston's hockey and basketball arena.

Luckily, Boston has many special libraries, archives, and museums with paintings and old photos that captured Sarah's city. Insurance records told me which businesses she passed on her way to the Otis School; a newspaper sketch let me see her courtroom. I read about Sarah's case and times in newspapers, journals, court documents, Sumner's amazing speech, and history books, including a great one called *Sarah's Long Walk*.

Interviews helped too. One of Sarah's living relatives, Lena Reddick, told me how Sarah was educated while awaiting her court date. Reverend Franklin A. Dorman identified her whereabouts as she grew older.

I also talked with Linda Brown's sister Cheryl Brown Henderson, cofounder of the Brown Foundation. We discussed how important it is to make complicated issues clear without reducing them to simple answers. Part of her life's work has been to correct misunderstandings about *Brown v. Board of Education of Topeka*'s history: while the case bears Linda's family name, the Browns were actually just one of many families the NAACP brought together in this big step toward change. I tried to emphasize that fact in this story.

Unlike *Brown*, the Roberts case was named after them because Benjamin Roberts and his family were acting alone. But they were inspired—and supported—by those who were working for change around them. Boston was a city where many people, black and white, fought against slavery and for civil rights, including better education for African American children.

TRYING TO GET AT THE TRUTH

Sometimes, despite all efforts and research, parts of a story remain cloudy. We don't know, for example, whether Sarah was at her trial. I think it is most likely that her parents took her, which is why I put Sarah in the courtroom. Here are my reasons: Benjamin and Adeline Roberts wanted to challenge an unfair law. So they placed their daughter in an all-white school, knowing she might well be expelled. They also probably knew that it would be better to have Sarah sitting in court as a reminder that the case was about a real person (a common legal strategy). If they were willing to let their four-year-old experience being thrown out of school, wouldn't they bring a more mature seven-year-old to court where she'd be surrounded by her family—especially if it could help win the case?

I was most convinced, however, by the line in Charles Sumner's speech, "This little child asks at your hands her personal rights." *This little child.* Sumner spoke as if Sarah was right there with him.

Nonetheless, I wouldn't feel comfortable including something I wasn't 100 percent sure of without telling you it is an educated guess. *What would you have done if you were me?*

THE RIGHT WORDS MATTER

I don't usually use modern words in a historic story because they can jolt readers out of the past. The term *African American* didn't exist in 1847. But words used to describe African Americans 150 years ago feel insulting now, even the ones that were respectful then. So I wrote to historians, who agreed *African American* was the best phrase to use. For example, Lonnie G. Bunch III, director of the Smithsonian National Museum of African American History and Culture, said that it's important for African American kids to feel connected to their history. It's easier for them to relate to their ancestors if they share the name African Americans and put all belittling names behind them.

ONE STORY, MANY MESSAGES

What is this story about? And why did I want to write it? Was it to show the injustice of a child walking past five schools she couldn't enter to get to one she did not want to attend? Or to show that fighting for a cause can be a victory even if you lose? Or that the push to integrate schools started long before the 1950s? For me, it includes all these ideas, and especially the message that sums them up: If you feel something is wrong, speak up. And keep trying. Change happens when people of all kinds find a way to come together. *If you were telling this story, what idea would be most important for you?*